Cecelia's Gerbils

CECELIA'S GERBILS

A Story for Boys and Girls

A Manual for Adults

J. James Hasenau

An Exposition–Banner Book

EXPOSITION PRESS   NEW YORK

EXPOSITION PRESS INC.

50 Jericho Turnpike   Jericho, New York 11753

FIRST EDITION

LIBRARY OF CONGRESS CATALOG CARD NUMBER: 70–114065

0-682-47093-7

To our son, John, who raises

GERBILS

and who inspired this effort.

Contents

Part 1
A Story for Boys and Girls

Cecelia's Gerbils

Alfonso was cute and curious. He is the pet of Cecelia, a little girl who loves him very much. He looks like a small teddy bear, a little larger than a full-grown mouse. Cecelia got him from a pet shop when he was two months old.

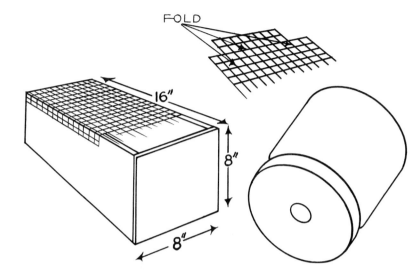

Simple Wood Box Cage
With Cold Cream Watering Bottle

Cecelia's father made Alfonso a little box out of wood. It is the size of a shoe box, and has paper inside for Alfonso to chew up and make into a nest. The wire top has a frame around it, but if the wire is stiff enough he wouldn't need a frame. Cecelia placed a cold-cream bottle with a hole in the top upside down on the wire for water. The pet-store man showed her a small glass aquarium that she could use with a wire top and water bottle. The aquarium would let her watch Alfonso more easily through the glass sides.

Cecelia fed her gerbil bread, cereal, grass, alfalfa and a few sunflower seeds, which Alfonso considered a treat because he would eat them first. The pet-store man had packaged feed for her too.

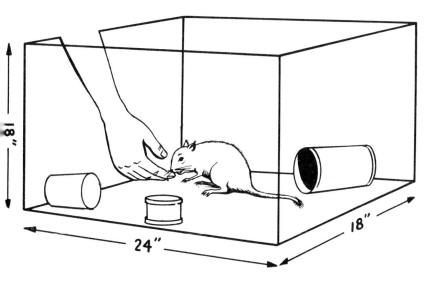

Alfonso was very curious about everything and would examine Cecelia's hand when she put it into the cage, or any other object, like a piece of wood, paper cup or spool. He was very gentle and when Cecelia picked him up by the tail, she could cup him in her hands and stroke his back. A small tomato can was Alfonso's favorite toy. He would crawl in and out of it all day long.

Cecelia bought Miranda when Alfonso was three months old. They got along real well together and after four weeks surprised Cecelia with two little red babies. Alfonso was surprised, too, because the stork usually doesn't visit gerbils so rapidly. It often waits for over a year. Sometimes, though, six children arrive all at once and as often as every twenty-four days. If this happens, Cecelia must give Miranda some bread soaked in milk to help feed all the little ones. Soon the babies will start nibbling on the bread and milk themselves. After about twenty-one days, they can say good-bye to Alfonso and Miranda and be on their own.

One day Alfonso got out of his home when Cecelia's brother left the top of the cage open. Cecelia got her father's flashlight and shone it into the dark corners and under the couch where she thought Alfonso could be hiding. Sure enough, Alfonso, under the couch, was so curious about the light that he walked right up to see what it was, and Cecelia picked him up by the tail and put him back into the cage with Miranda.

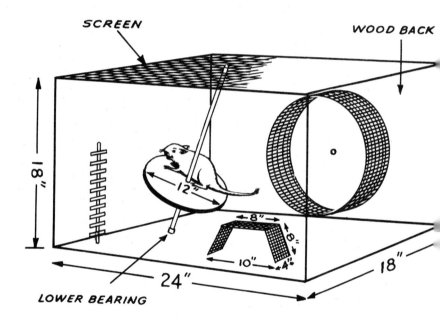

SCREEN

WOOD BACK

18"

24"

18"

12"

8"

8"

10"

4"

LOWER BEARING

Soon Cecelia had more of Alfonso and Miranda's babies than she wanted, so she gave some to her friends. Her father made an exercise cage with little ladders, poles, and a wheel for the gerbils to play on. Everyone enjoyed watching the playful things they did on the ladders and wheels.

Alfonso and Miranda are still living happily after three years and now have many grandchildren, all of whom are clean and healthy. They didn't even have winter colds or any kind of infection, fleas, or mites like other animals sometimes have. And Cecelia had a hard time loving all of them because there were so many.

Part II
A Manual for Adults

1.   Where to Get Your Gerbil

"Gentle Gerbil" is the coined word that best applies to the popular Mongolian gerbils. They are the size and weight of a large mouse and look like a fluffy little teddy bear. Their gentleness, cleanliness, and the fact that they do not have the disagreeable odor of most animals, make them highly desirable for pets and research. In the East, people pronounce the name "jurbill," and in the central states and West "gerbill." They are a new animal, the first one being imported to the United States from Japan in 1954. As soon as there are enough animals available, they will probably surpass the hamster and mouse in popularity. A pet store will have young animals paired off, so that they will be tame and gentle with one another and easy to handle. If you buy an older animal be sure to get a pair that have been together, or one by itself. Otherwise the fighting and adjustment among the animals, if old and young are mixed, will discourage a potential pet keeper.

Of course, if the animal is listless or tired-looking, with matted fur or running eyes, it is probably sick and should not be purchased. An active, curious animal is usually a healthy one, and will be running around the cage interested in everything. Gerbils are a fun animal to watch and will stand up on their hind legs to look around, something like squirrels or prairie dogs do.

2. Handling Gerbils

Handle animals by picking them up by the base of the tail, not the end, as the skin is thin there and may slide off. To pick up small babies with eyes just open, cup the hand and with scooping-up action gather them up like groups of marbles. Keep other animals away, such as cats, dogs, racoons; the gerbils will end up on the losing end. They are small, delicate creatures and one must be careful to handle them gently and not put too much pressure on them. Sometimes when one escapes, people get excited and capture it too vigorously.

The more one handles his gerbils the better they will adjust to people. However, any loud noises, sudden movements or extremely difficult situations cause excitement and nervousness among them. Moving cages, cleaning, sudden noises or anything the colony is not used to, will cause a reaction much like an epileptic seizure in some animals. However, as soon as the noise has been subdued the animal recovers completely. Some of these seizures are quite grotesque, with the gerbil jerking and twisting into various postures—my twelve-year-old says "like modern teen-age dancers." Another frequent form the seizure takes is an extension of the front feet and the collapse of the rear feet and body with no movement at all. Recovery is usually within a few minutes. In the thousands of animals we have handled, we have never been bitten to the point of having blood drawn. The most we have experienced has been a small nibble.

Transporting gerbils by air, car, or whatever method over a long distance for several hours causes the animal to exhibit a tired, droopy, shocked look, often interpreted as pneumonia. Livestock people call this shipping fever. The stress caused by changing an animal's environment is much greater than changing his food or handler. A day without food or water, then moving him back to a regular routine, will cure the pneumonia-like effect.

Care must be taken to avoid insecticides around the gerbils, especially the small ones. The popular insect-repellant strip will kill them if they are too close to it. Of course, the effect of sprays or poison depends on how near the animals are to where it is used; the effect can run from sickness to death.

3. Habits

One of the most interesting things to observe in gerbils' behavior is their curiosity. They are absolutely fearless; a finger extended into a cage is instantly observed and explored. They will run and hide if not used to your presence, but will soon come out to see what is going on. One time hundreds of them standing on their hind legs lined up shoulder to shoulder against the outside of the transparent cages to see what was happening when we opened an outside door that had never been opened before.

Digging seems to be an instinctive need, for gerbils will spend hours scratching into the corner of their cage in a seemingly endless effort to dig out. This is quite a violent movement as it is rapid and vigorous, causing sawdust, food, bedding, babies, everything, to go flying. After a while it stops and the animal returns to normal activity. Digging is a frequent form of exercise occurring every two or three days.

Gnawing also seems to be a necessary activity. Any wood or plastic object will be chewed to pieces after a few weeks. If the cage wires are far enough apart, the animals will continually gnaw on the wire causing damage around their nose and head as they rub against the next wire. Loss of fur and a bloody nose are the net results. Many breeders place a block of hard wood, a piece of flooring, or small length of broom handle in the cage to keep the animals busy gnawing on it, rather than on the cage or food. Some animals need other things to do; an exercise wheel, tin cans, runways or bridges keep them busy. Otherwise, the animals often chop up the food for bedding or floor litter, pulling it out of the holders and spreading it around.

EXERCISE WHEEL

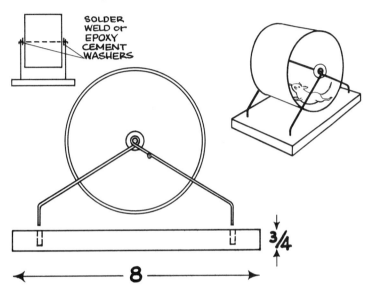

SOLDER
WELD or
EPOXY
CEMENT
WASHERS

3/4

8

MATERIAL:

Coat Hanger Wire
Coffee Can about **4**"across
Lumber, ¾"× 8 × 8
Two Washers with hole the size of
coat hanger wire ⅛"

EXERCISE DISC

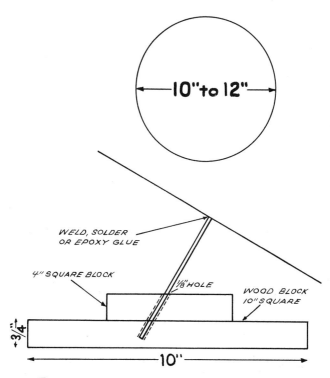

MATERIAL:

24 Gauge Galvanized Iron Coat
Hanger Wire • ¾"x10"x10"and ¾"x4"x4" Pine

EXERCISE DISC

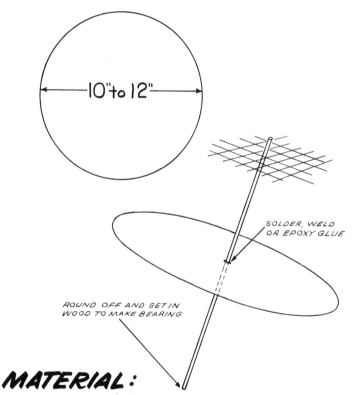

10" to 12"

SOLDER, WELD
OR EPOXY GLUE

ROUND OFF AND SET IN
WOOD TO MAKE BEARING

MATERIAL:
Coat Hangar Wire·10" to 12" Square
of Galvanized Iron or Sheet Metal

BRIDGE

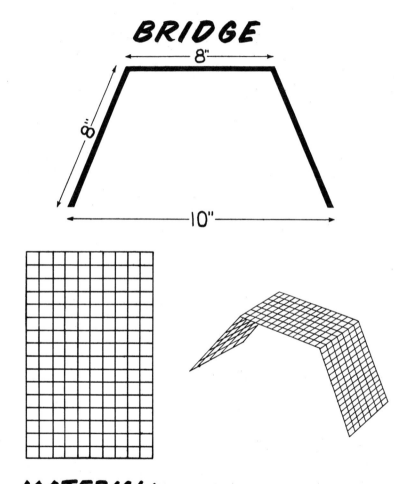

MATERIAL:
½"or 1"Hardware Cloth or Mesh

LADDERS

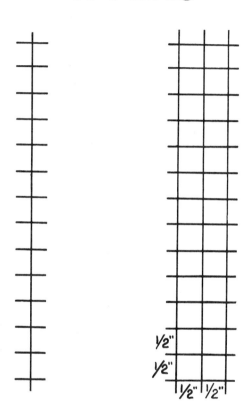

½"
½"
½" ½"

MATERIAL:

½"or1" Hardware Cloth or Mesh

Baby gerbils will squeak when they are first born and up to weening. Adults will thump with their hind legs with a thump, thump, thump rhythm. At times the whole colony will do this in perfect unison. We don't know what it means, but our guess is that it must be a way of communication among the animals.

Gerbils are nocturnal animals; they sleep all day and are most active at night. Our colony is quite active during the day too, but individuals and groups of animals often ball up and sleep for short periods either day or night.

4. Caging Gerbils

The best type of caging is a shoe-box style cage, available in plastic or porcelain, the same as a dish pan one would buy from the local five-and-dime or hardware store. It has rounded corners which are easy to clean. A wire top allows for air circulation and will hold an inverted water bottle. If the wire top isn't too high from the floor of the cage, a cold-cream jar with a hole in it, or a sipper tube in a rubber stopper, available at pet supply stores, also makes an ideal watering arrangement. The wire can be spread apart with a ball-point pen shoved down into the wire and twisted to enlarge the hole enough to receive the sipper tube. This is a 3/16″ diameter steel, copper or glass tube. Good commercial ones are stainless steel. Gerbils and hamsters, when first introduced into this country, didn't take water as such, but obtained enough moisture from fruit and greens to survive. Today's animals have evolved to the point where they need water to live. They have learned to drink water and can no longer depend on greens and moisture in food to satisfy their thirst. At least this is true of the strains with which we are familiar. Most of today's pellet diets are dry, and water is a necessary element.

Aquariums are inexpensive, readily available from pet stores, and offer the additional caging advantage of complete visibility. Some aquariums are deep enough that they won't need a top, however, it is usually best to use a wire top. The sipper tube or water system will have to be extended to within an inch or two of the cage bottom. In this case, the bedding or sawdust must be kept light or low for the gerbils, who digging around in the bedding material will cover the sipper tube and all the water will

DISH PAN CAGE

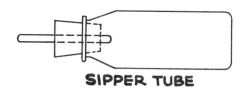

SIPPER TUBE

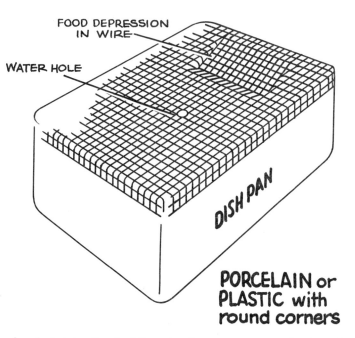

FOOD DEPRESSION
IN WIRE

WATER HOLE

DISH PAN

**PORCELAIN or
PLASTIC with
round corners**

be absorbed into the bedding, leaving no water to drink and a wet cage floor with possible sick or dead animals. A water bottle holder can be bent out of 2″ strip sheet metal to lower the regular bottle nearer to the floor of the aquarium. Food racks can also be suspended over the side of the cage by using wire or sheet metal strips. A plan is suggested for cold-cream style water bottle holders in aquariums, using a coffee can as illustrated.

AQUARIUM TYPE CAGE

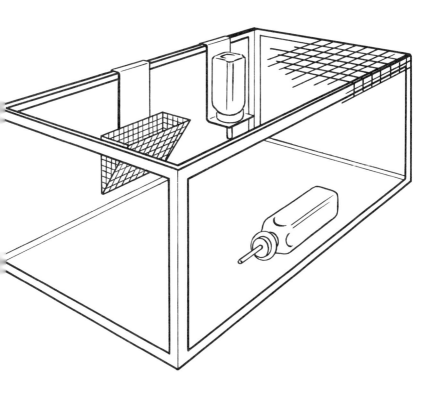

WATER STAND
For Deep Aquarium

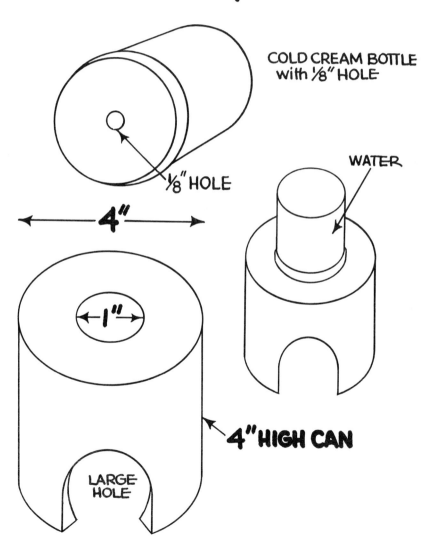

COLD CREAM BOTTLE
with ⅛" HOLE

⅛" HOLE

4"

1"

WATER

4" HIGH CAN

LARGE
HOLE

SHOW TYPE CAGE

Styled after mouse show cages used in exhibiting for competition in England.

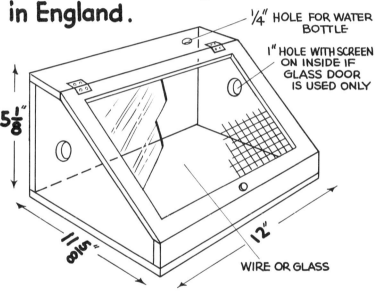

¼" HOLE FOR WATER BOTTLE

1" HOLE WITH SCREEN ON INSIDE IF GLASS DOOR IS USED ONLY

5⅛"

11⅝"

12"

WIRE OR GLASS

MATERIAL :
¾" × 11⅝" × 36"   Pine
¾" × 1⅝" × 24"   Pine
¾" × 3⅝" × 12"   Pine

WOOD BOX CAGE

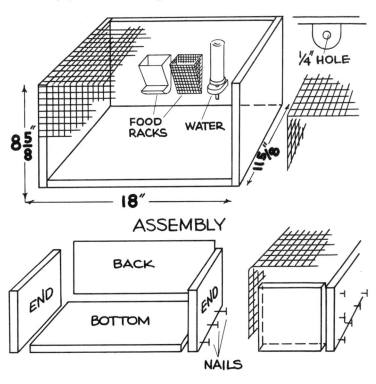

¼" HOLE

8 5/8"

FOOD RACKS   WATER

18"

11 5/8"

ASSEMBLY

END   BACK   END

BOTTOM   NAILS

MATERIAL :
¾" × 11 5/8" × 5"   Pine
Hardware Cloth 18" × 2 Feet ¼" Mesh
Screw Eyes ¼"

Wooden box type cages have advantages. An 8″ x 16″ floor area about 8″ high is sufficient for two gerbils or a breeding pair and litter. Use either a wire or wood top. If one uses a wooden top, the box must have wired-over holes on the end or side to provide ventilation, that is, two holes, one on each end or one on each side. A wire top will accommodate a cold-cream water bottle. A nesting part can be partitioned off at one end, although the gerbils will build their nest any place in the cage, not necessarily where the nest box is. A wooden box offers a variety of size possibilities for litters of different groups.

One style cage has floor, back and sides of wood. A mesh wire bent L shape forms the front and top. A small door can be installed hinged and flush so that the animals cannot get a purchase to gnaw out. If they do the area affected can be covered with wire mesh or reinforced with tin plate. A medium-size gerbil can crawl through a one-inch hole; if they can get their head through, the rest of the body looks large but is all fur and it will go through too. Any painting inside the cage should be with non-toxic paint especially made for baby furniture; the outside makes no difference. Lead-base paint can quickly kill gerbils. A cookie pan or square cake pan is an ideal base to build the cage around. It will keep the urin and droppings from soaking into the wood, eventually causing a disagreeable odor.

Commercial style cages are too open and the gerbils throw all the bedding and food out through the wires.

Wood lends itself to artistic shapes, castles, Old Woman in the Shoe or two-story houses with stairways and picture windows, so that one can watch the animals run around inside. The wood has warmth, in that it doesn't change temperature as fast as steel pans, plastic or glass. Gerbils withstand and adjust to a wide variety of temperatures and humidity. Freezing is the lowest temperature the animals can stand, but this only with good bedding and neighbors. Wood does not clank or give off as much noise as the other type of cages.

A gerbil must feel like it is inside a drum when two metal cages hit against one another. This can cause extreme excitement.

COMMERCIAL TYPE CAGE

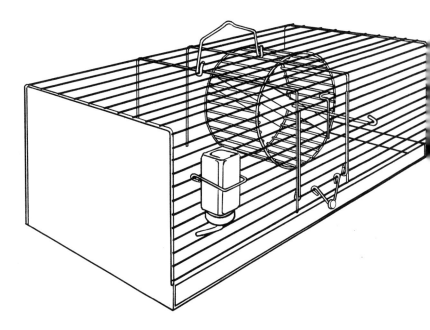

COMMERCIAL BREEDING CAGE

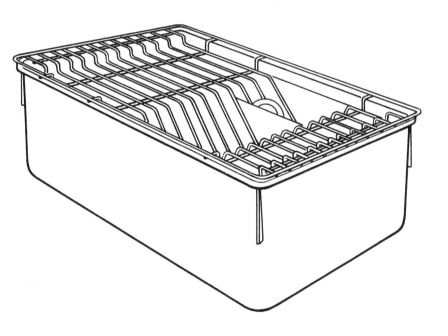

CAGE

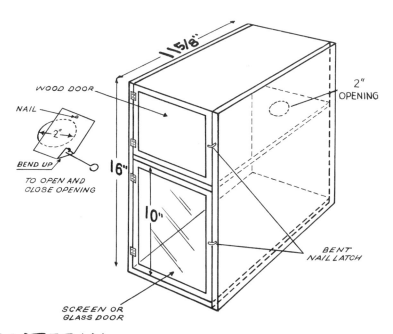

MATERIAL:

¾"x 11 ⅝"x 6' Number 1 Pine •4 Small Hinges • 6 Penny Finishing Nails • 5"x 8 Glass or 5"x 8" Screen

Mothers may kill babies, or carry them from one end of the cage to the other, eventually killing them. The wood cages offer insulation against outside noise and visual stimulation. Wood is cheap and available. Sometimes, especially after having babies, the animals get disturbed if they see someone or something. An old towel or piece of rug over a box type cage offers protetcion against the noise, cold and moving objects.

Wooden cages have certain disadvantages however; they are difficult to clean and absorb odors and moisture excessively. Several manufacturers have non-toxic plastic paint that will work on the wood cages to control odor and moisture absorption, especially on the bottom where urine drops may collect. With this type of paint it isn't necessary to come up the sides more than half an inch or so to protect the bottom of the cage, wood sides and corners. Make sure to cover all of the bottom of the cage.

5. Bedding

Sawdust is the most easily obtained bedding. But other things that will do are ground corn cobs, newspapers, wood shavings, sand, commercial kitty litter, and cedar shavings. Cedar shavings cause some skin rashes on younger animals and would be best avoided. Also, fine sawdust has a drawback in that suckling young eat it, often killing themselves. Sand and kitty litter tend to be dusty. These materials are thrown around violently as the gerbils dig in the corners. The dust comes out of the cage through the wire top or sides and makes a mess. Avoid cloth, anything that has thread in it, for the threads will entrap and strangle babies or even adults.

We use white pine shavings obtained from a local wood window company. It smells nice and fresh and absorbs moisture and odors. We pick up garbage cans full, thus relieving the window company of the task of burning or hauling the shavings away to a dump. If nesting material isn't available, the shavings will do.

6.   Nesting

A nest will be built by the gerbils if there are newspaper scraps or paper napkins in the cage. They will pull it all apart and make a round dish-shaped nest with the paper. If there is enough paper, the nest will be in the center of a large ball giving them complete privacy. This also tends to deaden sound and light.

Another good nesting device is a soup or bean can with one end cut out. The animals will gnaw on it and nest inside. This helps group the gerbils together and saves body heat in cold weather, although we keep our rooms at a constant heat. Drafts are also prevented by using this can nesting system.

7. Cleanliness

In general keep your pet's cage and water bottles clean and dry. Develop a habit of snapping the water bottle with the wrist to break the air lock in the sipper tube just before placing the bottle in the cage. If water drips from the tube on the floor and air bubbles group at the top of the bottle, water will flow easily when the gerbil sips on the tube. Watch that the bottle doesn't drip into the cage. This excessive dampness can quickly kill the gerbils. A clean cage means a dry bottom with sawdust or droppings and no decayed or moldy food mixed in with the bedding. Clean the cage by brushing out with a wisk broom or a stiff paint brush. Wash metal or plastic cages with soap and water.

Change cages in the wash tub or bath tub until your gerbils have become accustomed to you, and you to them. This cuts down their chances of escape. Sometimes they are nervous at cage-cleaning time, and will jump and run, especially the very young who are extremely nervous and quick to react. Older gerbils if they get out of a cage tend to just wait for you to pick them up and put them back. Of course use a slow, cautious approach. If you run at them, or use quick, noisy movements they become frightened.

Live catching cages are available through several mail order manufacturers who advertise in pet-store magazines or small-game-hunting monthlies.

Or, you can make a live trap:
Bait the live trap with grain and bacon or cheese. If there are any mice or other rodents about, you will catch them too. A large colony of gerbils will sometimes attract mice because of the quantities of food. So you'll catch loose gerbils—or whatever is around.

LIVE TRAP

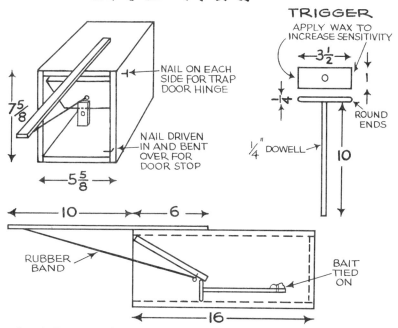

TRIGGER

APPLY WAX TO INCREASE SENSITIVITY

$3\frac{1}{2}$

$\frac{1}{4}$ DOWEL

ROUND ENDS

10

NAIL ON EACH SIDE FOR TRAP DOOR HINGE

$7\frac{5}{8}$

NAIL DRIVEN IN AND BENT OVER FOR DOOR STOP

$5\frac{5}{8}$

10 ― 6

RUBBER BAND

BAIT TIED ON

16

MATERIAL:

$\frac{3}{4} \times 5\frac{5}{8} \times 4$ Feet   No. 2 White Pine

$\frac{3}{4} \times 7\frac{5}{8} \times 4$ Feet   No. 2 White Pine

$1 \times \frac{1}{4} \times 2$ Feet Slat   White Pine

RUBBER BAND

SMALL SCREW EYE

6 PENNY FINISH NAILS

8. Determining Sex

Baby gerbils just born are the easiest to catagorize into male and female groups. The little red dots on the underside of the female are the testes. If there are no little red dots, the gerbil is a male. After about four weeks, the sexes are easily distinguishable by the shape of the body where its meets the tail. On the male the body is tapered into the tail. The female, where the tail meets the body, is more like a lollipop.

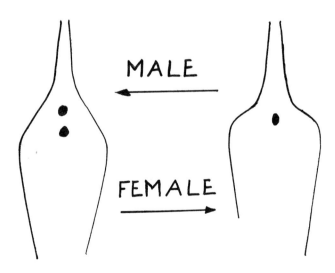

There is a short distance between the anus or rectum and the vulva or vagina in the female, making the openings appear as one; while in the male there are two distinct openings, the penis and the anus, which are approximately ¼ to ⅜ of an inch apart.

Determining sex is most important in breeding. Many an amateur is waiting for the first litter from two males or two females.

9. Breeding

The breeding period lasts all year and starts at ten to twelve weeks of age. Litters are from one to twelve, and take about twenty-four days to arrive. Immediately after the birth, the female is again in heat (fertility period or breeding cycle). This means that the female can be bred again at this time. Close to sixty per cent of the females can be bred or drop a new litter twenty-five days after the first litter. Heat periods last about four days and occur approximately every six weeks. The female will continue to breed for almost two years.

Dominant females around six months old will often kill a new male introduced into the cage. For this reason, mating must be started early. The plan we follow is to take two females for each male, the male being from a different litter. We wean at twenty-five to thirty days, then hold the sexes separate and pair at nine weeks. This seems to give best results for reproduction. At this age they accept each other readily and get along just fine. However, at sexual maturity (age ten to twelve weeks) if animals are mixed up or mated, they will occasionally fight to the death. The female is so selective of her mate at a later age that she very seldom accepts a male. If something happens to her first mate she may not breed, even though she will live with and not fight another male. Young males and females, twenty-five to a cage, weanlings, get along quite well for a while. Even then as they get older, individual aggressive fighters can be spotted and removed before they damage other animals. Injuries suffered in fighting tend to heal themselves once the fighters are removed to another cage. But often the gerbils, if not separated, will mutilate or kill one another.

In breeding, the most frequent complaint we have heard is the lack of it. Gerbils are slow breeders probably because of in-line, or closed colony, brother and sister mating carried to extremes. This is easy to realize if a person starts with a brother-sister group. Occasionally pairs are together over a year before they breed. A fertility period in the female occurs right after the babies are born. This is why the male will vigorously pursue the female immediately after she drops the litter. If one observes that the action becomes so vigorous that the female is unable to nurse or group the babies together we take the male out for a few days. When we put the male back he will help sit on the young, taking turns with the female or females to keep the babies warm. The other female will help, too, adding her body heat to the nest.

Outbreeding is the mating of unrelated stock, and is the best for maximum livestock production. However, in this process the gerbil loses its genetic similarity. Inbreeding tends to develop greater similarities in the animals. Inbred animals are preferred for research because of the need for animals that are all alike.

Another main reason for failure to breed is excessive weight in the male. A fat male gets lazy and refuses to get involved in breeding. If the male looks like a cute little teddy bear, he is too heavy to breed. A lot of sunflower seed can put on weight in a short time. We feed a prepared commercial four per cent, fat-content diet, with 17 per cent protein. It holds the weight down well.

New babies are little pink balls. They look like bugs; no teeth, no furs, no ears, and eyes closed. At five days dark fur is observed. In two and one half weeks teeth form, and ears form, and eyes open. They will eat solid food at seventeen to twenty-one days. On the twenty-fourth or twenty-fifth day weening is necessary to make room for the next litter.

Once babies are born wait three weeks before cleaning the cage. Most deaths of newborn babies seem to be from the new mother's excitement or the mother packing the babies or moving them from one corner of the cage to the other, seemingly trying to hide them. Also, the burrowing or frantic digging into the corners often sends babies flying and buries them in the shavings, sawdust or bedding. We dig them out and pile them in a corner, thus saving a litter. The mothers are so gentle that we have never known them to abandon or kill babies because we piled them all together or touched them. Mothers eating their own babies are rare but if it occurs it is probably caused by poor diet. Mothers with large litters sometimes put them into two groups, possibly to hide them, or divide the nursing time equally.

When a mother dies, is killed, escapes or abandons a litter we have successfully foster-mothered the litter by placing them in the care of another mother with a small litter of almost the same age. We first rubbed the babies' butts together with those of the new litter; this is supposed to give all the young the same smell, and the mother can't tell the difference. In our colony it works fine.

Large litters are watched and the mother is fed bread soaked in milk, the bread about the size of a dime. Then later, before the babies are weaned, place bread and milk on a piece of wood to keep it clean and the young will suck on it, relieving the mother. Long sipper tubes and soft food can encourage the young to take water and food early. An eye dropper filled with milk will work, too. It also helps to wean early, in case of a mother's death, or if she runs out of milk—which can happen because of stress, excitement, or large litters. The gerbils are quite valuable and a little extra effort saves a lot of babies.

Long sipper tubes should only be used just before and a short time after weaning, to help relieve the mother and to get the babies weaned sooner. After that, they can reach short sipper tubes, or an upside-down cold-cream jar with a drip hole. If the long tube is left in the cage, sawdust or bedding will enter the tube and float to the top of the water. Enough of this will polute and ruin the water: often the material that floats up in the water bottle will get water-soaked, swell up, and settle back into the tube to plug it up. Our tubes have a 45° bend in them and are placed in two positions: first, while weaning, the tube is pointed straight down; then, when weaning is over, the breeder simply turns the bottle 45°, if the animal is capable of reaching the higher tube. The 45° turn raises the end of the tube away from the floor.

Records for breeding are interesting and can be kept on almost

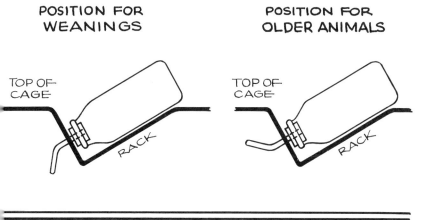

POSITION FOR
WEANINGS

POSITION FOR
OLDER ANIMALS

TOP OF
CAGE

RACK

TOP OF
CAGE

RACK

FLOOR OF CAGE

any genetic tendency. Weight growth charts are easy for children to keep. Records of good mothers and bad mothers, good tempers and bad tempers are important in a breeding program. The non-producing groups or individuals can be sold to laboratories.

As far as we know there are no color mutations as yet, but it will just be a matter of time; an albino will probably be first.

10. Food

As gerbils are grain, grass, root and seed eaters, food in the form of commercial pellets containing these is easiest to provide. Pellet food is best, as an apple or fruit tends to throw the diet off too much because it is usually given, or eaten, in excess. A four percent fat-content diet keeps the animal trim. A fat animal loses its ability or interest in breeding. The food must be provided in such a way as to prevent spoilage or contamination by the digging action described previously. Our most successful method is a wire box, of half-inch squares, hanging from the top or side of the cage. Bread, lettuce, or pellets placed in this are pulled through and eaten without getting soiled or mixed in with the sawdust or bedding. A grain-hopper is easy to make, it is designed to keep food off the floor of the cage. This is the only way to feed gerbils. Food or water in pans or crocks immediately becomes soiled, spilled, or mixed with the bedding. Sometimes the cage top of one-half-inch wire hardware cloth can be bent down into a pocket to hold food.

A good cage, food, and water set-up can be loaded with supplies and keep several gerbils for a week without any attention. This is an ideal vacation plan. You don't have to bother the neighbors while you're away; your pets will take care of themselves.

Care should be taken not to clean cages too often, every three weeks is sufficient, as gerbils eat a large amount of their own droppings to provide necessary vitamins. Gerbils, for this reason, cannot be raised on wire-bottom cages or self-cleaning cages, often used for mice, rats, rabbits, or mink. But by feeding a vitamin supplement gerbils can be raised on wire. A small piece of cabbage twice a week will work in place of the droppings or vitamin supplements.

Dog biscuits, regular commercial rat or mouse pellets and hamster food are ideal diets. Alfalfa and sunflower seeds add variety to the diet, but remember sunflower seed will fatten the animal.

It is worth while to watch for insecticides on lettuce, which will cause diarrhea. The gerbil will get better by itself, but one must watch for sickness, and change feed to control it. From all practical standpoints the gerbils are disease free.

FOOD HOLDER
For Lettuce, Alfalfa or Fruit

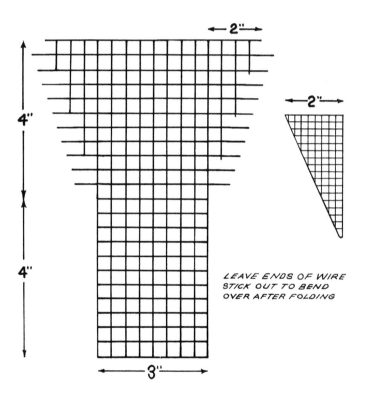

LEAVE ENDS OF WIRE
STICK OUT TO BEND
OVER AFTER FOLDING

MATERIAL:
½" Hardware Cloth or Mesh

FOOD HOLDER
For Dry Food

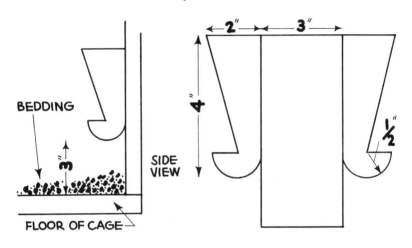

BEDDING

3"

FLOOR OF CAGE

SIDE
VIEW

2" 3"

4"

½"

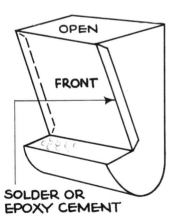

OPEN

FRONT

SOLDER OR
EPOXY CEMENT

MATERIAL: **TIN PLATE**

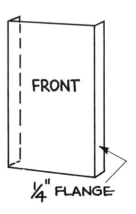

FRONT

¼" FLANGE

11. Games

These games are especially good for play school, nursery school, church carnivals, and even between two private participants they are fun. There are three races in which your gerbils can take part with sunflower seeds as rewards:

1. Using chalk, draw or lay string on the floor in a large circle 4 to 10 feet in diameter. Several circles make the race more exciting. A can in the center holds the racers. The starter lifts the can, and we watch to see who is first, second and third to reach the outer circle. To mark a racing gerbil use a felt-tipped marking pen. It will not hurt the fur and will wear off soon.

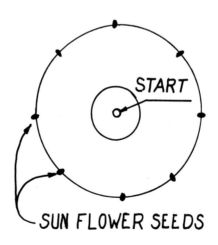

2. Set up a series of runs with a comb-like starting gate 4 or 6 feet long with about 2″ wide and 4″ high troughs. Again, put sunflower seed at the open end of the chutes. At the blocked-off end, use the comb-like starter to get them all off at once.

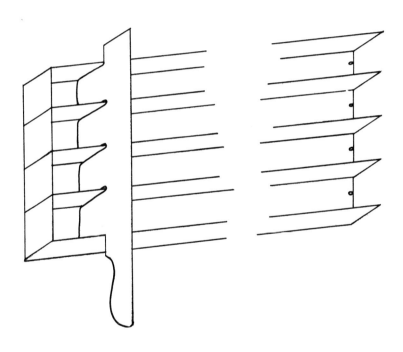

3. Design a maze to test your gerbil's memory and to see how fast it can reach the end. Gerbils are usually not good maze runners, being too curious to really concentrate on learning the maze.

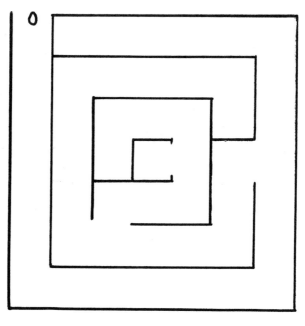

MAZE